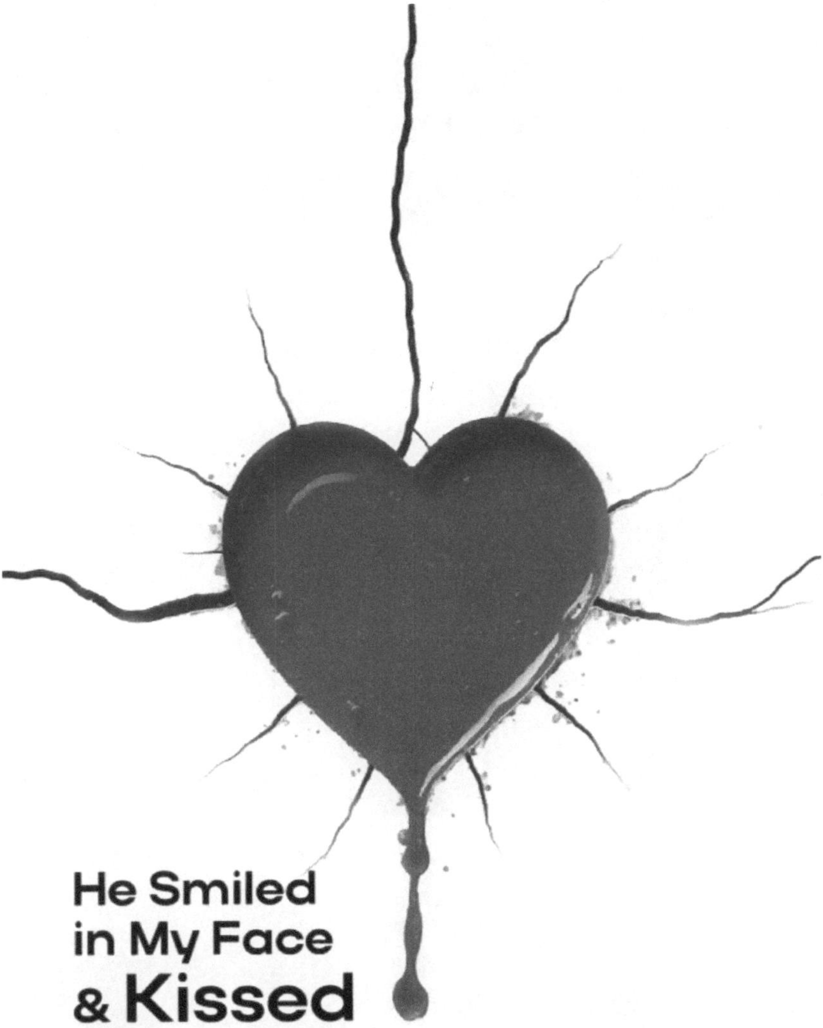

He Smiled in My Face & Kissed Me Like Judas

L'TANYA ARHEMAWORD *Publishing*

He Smiled in My Face & Kissed Me Like Judas

Author
L'Tanya P. Jones

To every Judas.

Thank you for rejecting me.

Thank you for denying me.

Thank you for deceiving me.

Thank you for betraying me.

Thank you for mistreating me.

Because you pushed me closer to God.

You forced me into purpose.

You revealed who I was.

You made me run to Him.

*And you will never take credit for
what He birthed in me.*

— L'Tanya

Contents

Author's Note

Before you turn these pages, I need you to know something.

When I first named this book *The Penis That Hurt Me*, it was about my childhood.

It was about the sexual abuse I experienced as a little girl.

I was going to tell it all—every traumatic detail.

Because that's what I thought healing looked like.

But God took this book in a different direction.

He showed me that while that pain shaped parts of me, it was never my identity.

And in His kindness, He didn't require me to relive it on these pages.

Because what hurt me as a child wasn't just a person—it was the silence that followed.

The grooming, the shame, the secrets, the words I never spoke . . .

That's what kept me bound.

So yes, this title started with my childhood story.
But this book is about every manipulation.
Every counterfeit love.
Every betrayal that followed.
I want you to know right now:
You are not what happened to you.
You are not what they called you.
You are not what they did.
You are God's daughter.

This book is my healing.
May it lead you to yours.

L'Tanya

Part 1

The Unraveling

1

Introduction to Judas: Where It All Begins

<hr>

I wasn't a teenager when it happened. I wasn't naive. I wasn't sheltered. I was a grown woman. A whole adult. And still, I got got.

I met him with a full heart and open arms, thinking I had finally found something real. But what I didn't know was that a grown woman can still be groomed. A woman with degrees, children, responsibilities, and wisdom—can still be groomed.

It didn't start with sex—it started with conversation. The smooth talk. The charm. The attention I didn't know I was still craving. He knew what to say, how to say it, and when to say it. And I—still healing from years of pain, disappointment, and survival—fell for it.

He studied me. That's what predators do. They don't pounce—they prepare.

He found my soft spots and pretended to protect them.

He learned my language and spoke it fluently.

He didn't just want my body—he wanted my loyalty, my silence, my submission.

And he got it.

In the beginning, worship was always on the agenda. He dressed the part . . . Bible in one hand, my hand in the other . . . reaching for what he knew mattered most to me. But little by little, I saw the mask slip. To me, his words said he believed, but the fruit of his life told a different story. He wasn't pulling away from me but from the very God he pretended to hold on to . . . withdrawing from everything that mattered, until faith felt like it was mine alone to carry.

Because the little girl in me—the one who still needed to be chosen, protected, and cherished—believed him.

I thought I was in control. But I wasn't.

I thought I had standards. But I bent them.

I thought I knew what love looked like. But I had only seen its counterfeit.

This wasn't just about a man.

It was about what I hadn't yet healed in me.

That's how the abuse got in.

Not because I was weak.

But because I was still waiting to be loved the way I was meant to be.

And predators can smell that.

He didn't hit me. He didn't yell. But he knew how to dominate my mind.

He'd pull back just enough to make me chase.

He'd say just enough to make me stay.

He'd promise just enough to make me hope.

And then when I gave myself to him—not just physically, but emotionally, spiritually, financially—I felt it.

That shift.

Something inside of me broke.

Not all at once. But piece by piece.

Every time he lied.

Every time he left me questioning my worth.

Every time I defended him to myself and others.

I started to lose me.

And I didn't even realize it until much later.

That's the danger of emotional abuse—you don't always see the bruises, but you bleed just the same.

I played the role of the strong woman. The provider. The prayer warrior.

But deep down, I was begging to be chosen. And I didn't even know it.

And that's where it all started.

Not in the bedroom, but in the lie that I was supposed to prove I was worth loving.

This chapter may be hard to read.

But I had to tell the truth.

Because healing doesn't begin until the truth is told.

And my truth is this:

He never loved me. He used me. And I let him.

But that is not how my story ends.

2

When the Mask
Started to Slip

He didn't go to Baltimore.

He didn't go to New York.

But the lies traveled with him anyway.

There's a certain kind of tired you feel when your soul is screaming but your mouth is silent.

I remember standing in front of a hotel mirror . . . Baltimore . . . face beat, outfit laid, hair fresh. On the outside, I looked like I had it together. But inside I felt invisible.

We weren't arguing. We weren't even talking. And somehow that silence felt louder than any shouting match ever could.

That trip was supposed to be a reset. A recharge. But the only thing getting charged was my card.

I was carrying everything . . . the planning, the payments, the prayers.

Judas just showed up.

And somehow, even in my presence, I felt abandoned.

That's when the whispers started. Not from Judas . . . from God.

The kind that hits you between your ribs.

The kind that says, "You don't belong here."

But I wasn't ready to hear that.

So I did what I'd learned to do . . . I stayed.

Later that night, I gave him my body, hoping he'd give me something back.

He didn't.

Judas took what I offered, then rolled over like I was an afterthought.

And still . . . I stayed.

That wasn't the only trip. New York was next. Or maybe it wasn't. I don't remember the order anymore . . . just the emptiness they left behind.

Different city. Same silence. Same pattern. Same pain dressed in cologne and manipulation.

In between those trips were others—other men.

Not because I was healed but because I was hollow.

Sometimes the fastest way to forget one disappointment is to fall into another one.

So I did.

They weren't much better.

They smiled differently. Lied better. Made love worse.

Each one took something.

But what I couldn't admit back then was this: I handed it to them.

Because I didn't know what I was worth.

Because I thought sex might turn into safety.

Because I thought giving more would finally make someone stay.

But nobody stayed.

Not them.

Not Judas.

Not even me.

I had been gone for a while . . . just a body moving through life while my soul sat in the corner, arms folded, waiting for me to wake up.

And slowly, I did.

I started waking up. Not all at once . . . but enough to know that either I was going to change, or else this was going to destroy me completely.

I didn't want to pray the kind of prayer that moves heaven and shakes the ground . . . because I knew what would happen if I did.

I knew that if I truly submitted and asked God to break this, He would.

And I wasn't ready. Not because I didn't believe . . . but because I did.

I knew my gifts. I knew the power that moved when I got serious. So instead, I played it safe.

I started going back to church. Sitting in the pew. Singing the songs. Trying to ease my way back into God's presence.

But the minute Judas needed something . . . or manipulated the situation so I'd stay home, cancel plans, or be unavailable to the world . . . there went God. There went church.

And just like that, I was back in the cycle. Again.

Only this time . . . I couldn't unsee what I had seen.

I had signs I couldn't ignore. Proof in the shadows, whispers caught on the wind.

I saw traces of her in spaces that should've been mine alone. And still, I froze.

She marked her spot. And Judas let her.

All I could think was, how dare you?

How dare you sit in my face, eat my food, sleep in my bed . . . and put her in my seat like she belonged there?

But I didn't explode.

I didn't throw a scene.

I froze.

Because when disrespect becomes familiar, you don't even know how to react anymore.

And then there were the chains . . . the hunger Judas couldn't name, the thirst he couldn't quench.

He said it wasn't bondage. But it was.

And I lacked the courage to call it what it was. Because by then, I was already too numb to fight.

I heard Judas on the phone one day . . . laying out his escape plan.

Didn't know I was listening. Didn't care enough to cover his tracks.

He was cleaning out his things little by little. Setting himself up to leave.

And I just stood there.

I knew what I should've done. But I couldn't.

Because you can have all the evidence, all the truth, all the Spirit . . . and still not have the strength to walk away when your soul is tired.

People thought I had it together. Because of how I dress. How I talk. How I show up.

But behind closed doors, I was unraveling.

I had no one to tell. No one I trusted. No one who wouldn't judge me for falling for someone who never planned to catch me.

And that's when I had to ask myself the question I had avoided for years:

"What are you going to do now?"

Because Judas wasn't going to change.

And now that I saw him clearly, the only one left to face . . . was me.

3

I Fell for the One Who Told Me the Truth

He said it wasn't love. I didn't believe him.

He told me from the beginning what it was.

He never hid it. Never dressed it up. Never pretended.

And still . . . I believed something different.

Because when your heart is still bleeding from things you haven't named, even a half-truth can feel like a whole possibility.

We weren't related. But we were close enough that the lines should've never blurred.

And yet they did.

There had always been chemistry. Always a little something lingering in the air.

And when the opportunity came, I didn't walk away. I stepped in.

Not because I believed it was love . . . but because I believed I could handle it.

I thought I was strong enough to play it casual.

I thought I could keep my heart in check.

I thought I was finally the one with the upper hand.

But baby, that was a lie.

We started traveling together.

Sometimes I'd go to him.

Sometimes he'd come to me.

We shared cities, hotel beds, secrets, and shame.

We laughed. We drank. We explored.

But none of it was rooted in love . . . it was rooted in loneliness dressed up as excitement.

And when I gave him my body, I gave him more than I wanted to admit.

He didn't kiss much.

He didn't even try to make sure I felt anything.

But he sure expected everything from me.

Intimacy with him wasn't about connection. It was about control.

He took without giving.

He received without thinking twice about what I needed.

And that became the theme.

Once again, I was in something unbalanced.

Something silent.

Something that left me feeling empty while he walked away feeling satisfied.

I didn't speak up.

I told myself, "It's fine. At least he's honest."

But what I really meant was . . .

At least I wasn't alone.

For years . . . not months, *years* . . . I tolerated that dynamic.

Because it was familiar.

Because I knew what to expect.

Because I could pretend that casual sex didn't cost anything.

But it did.

It cost me my confidence.

It cost me clarity.

It cost me the version of myself that believed she deserved more.

He didn't owe me anything . . . and he made that clear.

But I owed myself truth. And I wasn't giving it.

Every trip, every silent moment, every time I ignored my own needs, it chipped away at the woman I was becoming.

Because deep down, I didn't want sex.

I wanted safety.

I didn't want a situationship.

I wanted significance.

But I was too afraid to ask for it . . . because I already knew the answer.

I cried silent tears after the passion wore off.

I cleaned the sheets and swallowed the shame.

And I still showed up for work, for family, for ministry . . . like I was okay.

But I wasn't.

And that's when God started asking me a question I couldn't ignore anymore:

"Why are you giving yourself to people who don't reflect Me?"

That hit different.

Because I had been doing all the right things—fasting, praying, speaking in tongues, journaling, repenting.

But the one thing I hadn't done was forgive myself for needing love so badly that I kept mistaking lust for purpose.

This man wasn't evil. He was broken . . . just like me.

But the difference was, he was honest about it.

I was the one trying to change the script.

He told me enough truth to hold me close . . . then kissed me like Judas.

So I stayed too long again.

4

When God Held the Mirror Up

Healing didn't start with them . . . it started with me.

I had done all I could in my own strength.

I'd fasted. I'd cried. I'd compromised. I'd performed.

But nothing broke the cycle . . . because I was still trying to fix it without facing myself.

So I did the one thing I had been avoiding:

I rededicated my life to God.

I didn't just say a little prayer.

I prayed a hornets' prayer . . . one my late pastor once taught me.

A dangerous, powerful kind of prayer.

The kind you only pray when you're ready to burn every idol and take your hands off the outcome.

I prayed, and I told God everything.

I repented.

I cried.

And I said, "God, do what I cannot do. I know You'll answer me—I just don't know if I'm ready for what that answer looks like."

And then . . . I moved.

I didn't go back to the church where my membership lived . . . I went where God led me.

And the sermon that Sunday It came straight out of James . . . the book about hearing the word and doing.

It felt like the preacher was talking only to me.

Every word hit.

And I knew: "God was holding the mirror up. I can't blame Him, or them, or the past. This is about me."

So I started doing what I knew to do:

- I turned off secular music.
- I walked through my house praying in tongues.
- I called on Jesus like I hadn't in years.
- I went old-school. That old Landmark faith.

And still… Judas was present under my roof. A body in the house, but no company for my soul.

Judas stayed, yes. But it was grudgingly.

A spirit in the house, but no company for my soul.

So I added something else to my healing: therapy.

I sat in front of a professional and asked the question I had never asked out loud:

"What's wrong with me that I keep accepting this?"

I was tired.

Tired of shrinking.

Tired of explaining.

Tired of looking like I had it all together when I was silently falling apart.

I finally told my sons.

Not the whole story at once . . . just enough.

Because I've always believed: Don't bring your children into something you're not ready to leave.

I had protected them from the truth.

Not because I was ashamed of them . . . but because I was ashamed of myself.

My sons see me as strong.

As honorable.

As someone who deserves the best.

And I didn't want to lose that in their eyes. Not for a man, not for my mistake.

But I couldn't hold it in anymore.

And when I told them, one of them gave me the truth raw.

Even my own house rose up with truth sharper than a sword: "Cast out the bondwoman and her son" (Galatians 4:30). It was as if heaven itself was confirming what I already knew.

I still made excuses.

I told myself, "Maybe I should wait. Maybe let the dust settle first . . ." But dust only covers chains . . . it doesn't break them.

And while I lingered in twilight . . . Judas was already moving in the shadows.

I overheard betrayal breathing through the walls . . .

an exit plan whispered like smoke . . .

a blueprint of leaving that didn't bother to conceal.

Heaven had already exposed it . . .

but fear kept me stuck.

Not because I doubted God . . .

but because I doubted me.

Then Saturday came—the day I swore I'd finally cast the lie out . . .

But provision didn't show . . .

and the shadow made the first move.

His departure was something I'll never forget.

What rose in my house that day was not love turned sour . . .

it was darkness unveiled.

It cursed . . . it slammed . . .

it hissed like the serpent

it had always been.

And over the chaos came one command . . .

"Be still. Do not move."

So I held my ground.

Praying under my breath . . .
pleading the blood . . .
covered only by the Name above every name.
The mask gathered its things . . .
the serpent slithered out with its secrets . . .
rolled its shadow through the garage . . .
and vanished into the night.
I said nothing . . . because God had sealed my mouth.
And when I opened the door . . . Judas was gone.
Gone for good.
Not by my strength . . .
but because God did what I asked Him to do . . .
He did what I could not.

5

Rebuilding Without the Lie

And that's where rebuilding began . . .
not with another man . . .
not with another distraction . . .
but in the silence after the serpent slithered out.
If I wasn't who they said I was . . . who am I now?
I didn't know that healing could hurt worse than the relationship.
I didn't know that being free could still feel like grief.
But I was done surviving.
It was time to rebuild . . . from the ground up.
This time, there were no distractions.
No man to call.
No drama to decode.
No games to play.
Just me. My silence. My Savior. And a storm of emotions I didn't know how to name.
I wasn't going to fake it this time.
I cried in my car.

I cried in the shower.

I cried at work . . . behind my smile and in between patients.

Because even though I was functioning, I was still bleeding.

But I kept going.

Because something inside of me . . . stronger than my emotions . . . had decided:

"We're not going back."

And so I isolated.

Not as punishment but as preservation.

I was being set apart, not pushed aside.

I was being refined, not rejected.

And I began to starve the parts of me that used to feed on toxic love.

There were days I didn't sleep.

Nights I sat up watching sermon after sermon.

That's when Pastor Keion Henderson became my spiritual companion.

His words poured into places therapy hadn't reached yet.

His messages named the feelings I didn't know how to describe.

He became my voice when mine was still trembling.

I cried through "How to Heal."

Then "Let Them Go."

Then "You're Not Crazy, You're Called."

Each sermon unraveled another knot in my soul.

Each word showed me a little more of myself . . . not who I had been but who I was becoming.

At the same time, I tried to keep showing up for therapy.

But the sessions felt different now.

I was already several visits in, and we hadn't touched the surface of my real pain. We were still in the "getting to know you" phase.

But God was already breaking yokes in the middle of the night while I wept on my couch watching YouTube sermons.

And I started to wonder if maybe . . .

Just maybe . . .

Jesus had become my therapist.

Because even though my human counselor had said powerful things—

Even though his own testimony moved me—

Even though he looked at me and said, "You *have* to write a book"—

The truth was . . .

God had already started writing it.

Through every tear.

Through every sleepless night.

Through every prayer I couldn't finish.

Through every Bible verse I read on that app with trembling hands.

God was peeling off the labels.

God was untying the lies.

God was rebuilding the foundation—without the cracks.

I didn't even know what to call this version of me.

But I knew she was new.

I was reading my Bible.

I was praying differently.

I was worshipping with a desperation I hadn't felt in years.

And I wasn't doing it for a blessing.

I wasn't doing it to earn peace.

I was doing it because my soul was hungry—and God was the only one feeding me.

6

Restoration Is My Portion

Falling in love with Jesus—and leaving religion behind

I grew up in churches—a lot of them.

We went to so many, it felt like we switched pews every five minutes.

I promised myself as a child:

When I'm grown, I won't be running in and out of churches like this. I want keep moving, I won't keep searching.

But what I didn't realize then was that I was searching for God in buildings that never taught me how to truly find Him.

They told me what not to wear.

They told me where I couldn't go.

They told me what not to say.

But they never really told me how to love God.

They taught me rules. But they didn't teach me relationship.

And if someone did teach me, it didn't stick.

Because what stuck was this:

Fast for forty days . . . get a breakthrough.

Pay a ten percent tithe . . . get financial increase.

Go to church for fifty-two Sundays . . . your man will come.

And because I was faithful . . . I expected results.

It was transactional.

Just like my relationships with people.

I didn't even realize I had built my entire life on this give-to-get mindset.

Until God stripped it all.

And that's when I learned:

"You're not here to serve ME to get something. You're here to know ME. To love ME. To be Mine."

That revelation didn't come in a sermon.

It came in a shift.

In the early mornings, God kept waking me up.

When I hadn't slept.

When I'd cried myself to exhaustion.

When I thought I had nothing left . . . God breathed on me.

And I'd reach for my Bible app. Or my journal. Or whatever message He led me to.

And without realizing it . . . I was spending three to four hours with Him daily before I even brushed my teeth.

God became my first thought.

My safe place.

My joy.

My truth.

My love.

And one day, a song I had heard dozens of times came on . . . "Falling in Love With Jesus" by Jonathan Butler.

I use to hear it and think it was beautiful.

But this time? It hit different.

I felt it in my spirit.

Like I finally knew what it meant.

Because I wasn't in love with any man.

I wasn't in love with attention or affection or performance.

I was in love with Jesus.

And for the first time in my entire life, I think I felt something real . . . something I couldn't fake, something I never felt even in my most romantic relationship.

I was loved.

Covered.

Chosen.

Held.

Not for what I did.

But because of who I was to Him.

And I said out loud:

"Lord . . . I don't think I've ever been in love before. But now? I think I finally know what it feels like."

7

I Said What I Said

I didn't even know I had boundaries—because for most of my life, I didn't know I needed them or had the right to have them.

What I had instead was accommodation.

People-pleasing.

Over-giving.

Shrinking to keep the peace.

Saying yes when everything in me was screaming no . . . and calling that "love."

But it wasn't love.

It was survival.

It was trauma in a church dress.

That's when I learned the power of boundaries, boldness, and finally choosing me.

It was performance that looked like peace but felt like prison.

I used to think that being easygoing made me godly.

That being available meant I was loyal.

That being quiet meant I was mature.

But the truth was that I had no idea how to protect myself.

I didn't know the language for boundaries, because for years, I thought love meant access—even if it cost me everything.

And when I finally started naming my pain, something broke open in me.

That's when I said it:

I'm not doing this anymore. I don't owe anybody access to me. I'm not shrinking, not bending, and not explaining

I said what I said.

That phrase became my healing anthem.

Not in pride . . . but in clarity.

Because once I realized how many of my relationships were transactional, I finally understood why I kept ending up empty.

People weren't loving me . . . they were using the space I kept leaving wide open.

They were filling their needs while I silenced mine.

They were writing checks with my time, my money, my body, and my emotional energy . . . and I was over drafting trying to keep up.

And here's the part that wrecked me:

My past didn't just hurt me. It formed me.

All the things I didn't deal with—the childhood adversity, the abandonment, the silence, the need to be chosen—it trained me to accept what I never deserved.

So to even call it "trauma" today? That's deliverance.

Because for years, I didn't even know it *was* trauma—I thought it was life.

I didn't announce my healing.

I didn't post about my boundaries.

I didn't argue, debate, or explain them.

I just made the shift.

Because real healing doesn't beg to be understood.

It just shows up different . . .and dares you to cross the line.

And once I realized I had never truly protected myself, I stopped trying to protect people from the consequences of their own behavior.

I no longer entertain back-and-forths.

If I've spoken in truth, in love, and with clarity . . . that's it.

You don't get multiple versions of my boundary.

You don't get to negotiate with my discernment.

You don't get to circle back when I've already shut the door.

I used to leave it cracked . . . just in case.

Just in case they changed.

Just in case they apologized.

Just in case they finally saw me.

Not anymore.

That door is closed, and so is the window.

Because I've learned that when you don't own your boundaries, you'll resent everyone who crosses them . . . even though you left the gate open.

And yes . . . it's even extended to my children.

Not because I love them less.

But because I finally love myself more.

I had to shift how I show up, how I respond, and how I allow myself to be involved.

I now choose peace over performance.

Discernment over guilt.

Email over emotional spirals.

Silence over saving.

Even financially, I got clear.

I used to feel obligated to rescue people, to show up because I could, to fix what was broken even if I didn't break it.

But I don't do loans anymore.

And if I ever do again, it's dollar-for-dollar: $100 borrowed, $200 returned.

And right now? My lending window is closed.

I'm not apologizing for that.

I'm not overexplaining that.

I'm not debating that.

Because here's what I now know for sure:

I'm not harsh.

I'm not distant.

I'm just not available for anything that costs me my clarity, my calling, or my communion with God.

8

A New Beginning— For Real This Time

When God confirmed my freedom and gave me the go-ahead to live again, I moved.

Physically.

Spiritually.

Emotionally.

Not just to a new place—but to a new place in God.

The old version of me would've still been explaining, still trying to prove why I needed to go.

But not this time.

This time, I didn't wait for approval.

I didn't ask for validation.

I just obeyed.

Because when God says "go," you don't need a committee vote.

You just need the faith to move.

And I moved.

I relocated.

I started living within my means.

I gave myself permission to rest, to breathe, to think again without the weight of manipulation and emotional warfare.

I said no to distractions.

No to fake support.

No to performing.

And yes—to me.

To peace.

To quiet mornings and answered prayers.

To starting over—for real this time.

Then came the "Cry Out Conference" 2025.

I didn't know what I was walking into—but God did.

And the moment I stepped into that atmosphere, I knew it was different.

This time, I wasn't attending from a place of desperation.

I was there as a witness.

As evidence of what happens when you finally let go of the Judas/Judette and the lie that you have to earn love through suffering.

That's when freedom starts. That's when healing becomes more than survival . . . it becomes testimony.

I saw women who still looked like what they'd been through.

And I saw myself—no longer bound by the same story.

I was free.

Not perfect.

Not healed in every area.

But free.

And then came the confirmation.

A phrase so tailor-made, so Spirit-led, that I knew heaven had placed it on the calendar just for me.

This wasn't a secondhand word. It came directly to me.

It came with the atmosphere—with the worship, the stillness, the divine hush that falls when God is about to make something official.

He said:

"You're not just out.

You're healed.

You're whole.
You're ready."
I didn't need another altar call.
I was already walking in it.
That day, something unlocked.
I felt the release.
The permission to live again. To love again—wisely, slowly, with God's leading.
To travel, to create, to build the vision HE gave me without shame or apology.
It wasn't a soft whisper this time.
It was a Kingdom mic drop.
God said:
"I was with you the whole time.
And now that you know Me for yourself—
Go.
Be.
Do.
Write.
Tell it.
Live it."
And I will.

27

Part 2

A Kingdom Assignment

9

No More Torture

There was a time when my mind was a prison cell. Not because the walls were locked, but because the same fears kept pacing inside it. I called it "waiting," but in truth, it was self-inflicted torture.

I waited on phone calls that never came. I waited for presence that never showed up. Even the porch became a witness—packages sitting there longer than love ever did. And when I packed my bags for trips, I carried knots in my stomach heavier than any suitcase. How could I lie next to a body and still feel the emptiness of absence?

That was my torment: not only betrayal, but the guessing. Always in my head. Always in my chest. It was like Pharaoh's whip—not just breaking the body but grinding down the spirit day after day. And still I stayed. Still I called it love.

But then came freedom. God didn't part the Red Sea for me—He parted the fog. One morning, I woke up and realized: I don't live there anymore. I don't live in suspicion, or torture, or silence. The anxieties that once tied me up in knots have no authority over me now.

And that realization brought tears. Not of sorrow but of gratitude. Gratitude that I survived the wilderness of suspicion. Gratitude that I can finally sit in my own home, pack a bag, book a trip, and not wonder what shadows are moving behind my back. Gratitude that the prison door was open the whole time—and that I finally walked through it.

God whispered, "Daughter, peace is not the absence of enemies. Peace is the presence of ME." That is how the torture ended.

Reflection Prompt

Where have you mistaken waiting for love? What anxieties have you carried that God never asked you to hold?

Declaration

I refuse to torture myself with suspicion. I will not live in fear of shadows. I choose peace over paranoia, freedom over fear, and truth over torment.

10

Vindicate Me

When the door finally closed behind Judas, I was left with nothing but silence. A silence so heavy it pressed against my chest. In those first days, I didn't have eloquent prayers or poetic words. My lips could only form three: "Vindicate me, Lord."

I wasn't asking for showmanship. I wasn't asking for public downfall. I wasn't even asking for repayment of what had been taken. My heart wanted vengeance, but my spirit knew better. I needed God to step in where I could not. I needed Him to prove that my tears were not wasted, that my labor was not in vain, that my name would not rot in the mouths of liars.

Scripture tells us, "Vengeance is mine, says the Lord; I will repay" (Romans 12:19). I clung to that promise the way a drowning soul clings to driftwood. Because in my flesh, I wanted to be the storm. But in my spirit, I surrendered.

Vindication did not arrive in the form I expected. There were no thunderclaps announcing justice. There was no parade celebrating my survival. Vindication came quietly—like manna in the desert. My peace was the proof. My healing was the headline. My freedom was the repayment.

Judas may have thought he walked away with the upper hand, but I walked away with the hand of God. And that was enough.

Reflection Prompt

Where have you prayed for vengeance when what you really needed was vindication? What would it look like to trust God to repay rather than trying to fight in your own strength?

Declaration

I release vengeance. I will not carry the burden of repayment. God is my defender, my judge, and my vindicator. My peace is my proof, and my healing is my headline.

11
Dream Deferred, But Not Denied

I used to think endurance was the same as love. If I could just hold on long enough, surely the dream would blossom. I told myself that what was deferred would not be denied. But in my waiting, I tethered the dream to the wrong vessel.

I longed for a family that looked whole, for children to have the father they deserved, for stability to cover us like a roof. And so I stitched my hopes onto a man who could not bear the weight of them. Like pouring fine wine into a cracked jar, everything I gave seeped away.

It wasn't the dream that betrayed me—it was where I anchored it. The Word says, "Hope deferred makes the heart sick, but a longing fulfilled is a tree of life" (Proverbs 13:12). My heart had been sick for years, not because the dream was wrong but because the foundation was.

And here is what I know now: God never asked me to shrink my dream to fit a counterfeit. The delay was not denial—it was redirection. What I thought was rejection was actually protection. The Father who numbers my days was not going to let me build a legacy on sand.

So yes, the dream was deferred. Yes, it sat heavy in my chest, a weight I carried through sleepless nights. But it was never denied. It is alive, waiting to be rooted in the right soil, at the right time, with the right covering.

And this time, I will not hand it to cracked jars.

Reflection Prompt

Where have you placed your dreams in the wrong vessel? How can you shift your hope from people who cannot carry it to the God who planted it in the first place?

Declaration

My dreams are not denied—they are preserved. I will not shrink what God gave me to fit what man cannot hold. I will wait for His soil, His timing, His fulfillment.

12

The Oil They Can't Carry

There was a season when I saw shadows of myself walking around in someone else. The jewelry I wore, the trips I took, the very rhythm of my life—echoed and imitated like a blueprint copied without permission.

At first, I thought it was mockery. Then I realized it was proof. Because counterfeits can only copy what is already authentic. The enemy has no creativity of his own; he can only recycle. Scripture says, "The thief comes only to steal and kill and destroy" (John 10:10). And so he steals patterns, borrows language, mimics movements. But he cannot originate.

So when I saw my reflection in places it didn't belong, I stopped grieving and started rejoicing. For if there is a duplicate, there *must* be an original. If there is a shadow, there must be light. And I am that original. I am that light-bearer.

It stung at first—yes, it hurt to see pieces of my life scattered in places they didn't belong. But then I remembered the tabernacle: God gave Moses specific instructions down to the cubit. No duplicate could carry His glory, because only the blueprint written by His hand could hold His presence. And so it is with me.

The world may copy my bracelets, my journeys, my steps—but they cannot carry my oil.

Reflection Prompt

Have you ever seen parts of yourself mirrored in others and felt diminished? What if, instead, you saw those reflections as proof that you carry something worth imitating?

Declaration

I am the original. I am the vessel God designed. No duplicate can carry my oil, and no shadow can dim my light.

13

Disrespected in Public, Gaslit in Private

There are wounds that come from behind closed doors, and there are wounds that cut deepest when inflicted in the open. I endured both.

I remember what it felt like to sit at a table and have my very name mishandled—called what I was not, as if my identity were interchangeable, disposable. And worse still, to hear laughter rise at my expense. To wear a crown in the Spirit yet be treated like a stranger in everyday life.

Then came the gaslighting—the turning of truth into smoke. Behind closed doors, what was obvious became denied, what was clear became blurred. Words twisted until I questioned my own sanity. One face in public, another in private. A living mask.

And then there was the public event. It felt like a banquet I was uninvited to. Seats were filled, toasts were made, futures announced . . .

and I was written out of the story as though I never existed. The humiliation burned like fire in my bones. Rage whispered, "Make them feel what you feel." I sat with destruction crouching at my door, ready to break open.

But God. Just as He warned Cain: "Sin is crouching at your door; it desires to have you, but you must rule over it" (Genesis 4:7). That night, God held me. He pulled me back from the edge, told me to be still, told me to live. What I thought would be my breaking became my testimony.

Now I see the gift in that rejection. To be misnamed only revealed that my true name was written elsewhere—etched in the palm of God's hand (Isaiah 49:16). To be dismissed only revealed that Heaven had already appointed me.

The gaslighting tried to make me doubt my worth. The banquet tried to erase my place. But light cannot be dimmed by lies, and destiny cannot be unseated by exclusion.

Reflection Prompt

When have you been misnamed, dismissed, or excluded? How might those moments have been divine redirection rather than destruction?

Declaration

I am not the names others gave me. I am not defined by the tables that refuse me a seat. Though rejected by men, I am chosen by Heaven, and my name is etched in His hands.

14

Always Something

Chaos became its own rhythm in that season. Just when I thought peace might breathe, another storm rose. Vacations cut short by sudden "sickness." Concerts delayed by unexplained detours. Promises of rest that turned into restlessness. It was always something.

It took me a long time to see the pattern: Disorder wasn't an accident . . . it was a weapon. The enemy thrives in confusion, and Judas was a willing instrument. Where there should have been joy, there was tension. Where there should have been laughter, there was silence. Where there should have been partnership, there was absence.

Scripture says, "For God is not the author of confusion but of peace" (1 Corinthians 14:33). If confusion is present, God is not the writer of that script. And so I finally recognized—if the pages of my life were filled with nothing but interruptions, it was because I had handed the pen to the wrong hands.

Looking back, I see it for what it was: The constant derailments were not coincidence. They were distractions meant to keep me weary, disoriented, and doubting my worth. Yet even in the "always something," God was steady. His Spirit kept whispering, "This is not what I planned for you. This is not peace. This is not love. Come out from among them."

And when I listened, the cycle broke. No more ruined vacations. No more sudden sicknesses. No more "always something." The soundtrack of my life shifted from chaos to calm.

Reflection Prompt

Have you mistaken constant drama for normal life? Where might confusion be keeping you from recognizing the peace God has already promised?

Declaration

I renounce confusion. I will not call chaos love. I choose partnership rooted in peace, not patterns of disorder. My life will not be defined by "always something" but by the steady rhythm of God's presence.

15

Snake in the Garden

In the beginning, I thought I had found good fruit. It looked pleasing to the eye, promising to the touch. I thought I had discovered what could satisfy my hunger. But like Eve in Eden, I learned the hard way that not everything is what it seems.

The snake was there from the start. He didn't slither in later—he was already coiled, waiting, watching. At first, he played the part of a protector, pausing his hiss to imitate truth. He spoke words that sounded like promises, but they were poison wrapped in honey.

I see it now—he never entered as a man ready to love, to build, to stay. He entered as a mask. Scripture says, "Satan himself masquerades as an angel of light" (2 Corinthians 11:14). What I mistook for light was only a disguise. What I mistook for love was only bait.

The betrayal was not a sudden fall—it was a slow uncoiling. Lies that seemed small, excuses that seemed harmless, masks that slipped only for a moment at a time. Until one day, the garden was bare, the fruit was spoiled, and I was left staring at the serpent for what he truly was.

But here is the victory: God never abandoned me in that garden. He walked with me through it, just as He did with Eve. And though I was deceived, I was not destroyed. Though the snake hissed, he could not silence my voice.

The same God who clothed Adam and Eve in their shame clothed me in strength. The same God who promised that the serpent's head would be crushed (Genesis 3:15) promised me that no deception would have the final word.

I walked out of that garden bruised, but I did not walk out alone.

Reflection Prompt

Where have you mistaken counterfeit light for love? What disguises do you need to unmask so you can see clearly?

Declaration

I will not be deceived by disguises. I will not eat spoiled fruit. I see the snake for what it is, and I walk in the victory of the One who promised to crush the serpent's head.

Part 3

The Legacy of My Yes

Legacy Declaration

This book is more than my story—it is my inheritance, my crown, and my testimony. What was meant to break me became the very ground where God birthed something eternal. Through betrayal, I found my voice. Through humiliation, I found my dignity. Through torment, I found my peace. Out of the ashes, I rose as a masterpiece.

This legacy is not measured in riches or titles but in words that will outlive me. Even when the earth passes away, these truths will remain. They are etched in black and white, to speak for generations yet unborn. This is my gift, my offering, and my testimony: that God is faithful to vindicate, to heal, and to crown His daughters with glory.

When I leave this earth, I leave behind more than memories. I leave behind a legacy—the written word of how God turned betrayal into breakthrough, pain into power, and silence into a song that will never die.

Declaration

I am crowned in victory. I am her who would never fail. My story is my legacy, and my legacy will live forever.

Final Reflection

If you made it to the end of this book, I already know something about you:

You were meant to.

This wasn't entertainment.

This was survival.

This was deliverance.

This was spiritual surgery.

I didn't write this because I had all the answers.

I wrote it because I needed healing.

And maybe—just maybe—you did too.

This book was never just about a man.

Or a breakup.

Or a situationship.

It was about every place where I gave myself away hoping to be seen.

Every place I tried to fix what didn't want to be healed.

Every time I confused being chosen with being used.

And if that's you too, I want you to know this:
You are not crazy.
You are not weak.
You are not too late.
The fact that you're still here means the enemy failed.
The fact that you can feel means your heart still works.
And the fact that you can cry? That means you're not numb anymore.
You're healing.
Even if it doesn't look like it.
Even if you still stumble.
Even if some days you want to go back.
Keep going.
Not to prove them wrong.
But to show yourself what it looks like to finally get it right.
With God. With yourself. With truth.
This is your healing.
This is your permission.
This is your freedom.
And if no one ever told you this before . . .
I see you.
I believe you.
And I'm standing with you.
L'Tanya

Final Prayer

Father God,

Thank You for every woman who picked up this book looking for answers but found You instead.

Thank You for not letting our pain be wasted.

Thank You for walking us out of deception and into deliverance.

God, I ask that You cover her.

The one who thought she was too broken.

The one who hid behind performance.

The one who gave everything and was left with nothing.

Remind her that she is not forgotten.

Remind her that she is still Your daughter.

Remind her that healing is her portion.

Break every soul tie.

Expose every hidden lie.

Uproot every seed planted by betrayal.

And replace it with truth. With wholeness. With identity.

God, show her who she is in You.

Not in her trauma. Not in her mistakes. Not in the opinions of others.

But in Your eyes. In Your love. In Your Word.

Let this be the season where she no longer settles.

Where she stops shrinking.

Where she walks boldly.

Where she loves wisely.

Where she prays without fear and worships without shame.

Restore everything the enemy tried to steal.

And let her rise in power.

Not because of who hurt her.

But because of who healed her.

In Jesus' name.

Amen.

L'Tanya

About the Author

L'Tanya is a prophetic writer, speaker, and Kingdom visionary who spent decades surviving betrayal, loss, and silent battles no one saw. Her raw storytelling and bold, truth-telling voice dismantle shame and empower women to confront what hurts, heal what's hidden, and rise into who God called them to be. Her writing style echoes the way she talks—honest, unfiltered, and deeply anchored in faith. *He Smiled in My Face and Kissed Me Like Judas* is her debut work, born out of the silence the enemy once used against her. Refusing to stay muted, she now tells the truth out loud to help women break free.

When she's not writing, L'Tanya is interceding, traveling, and living out her calling as an ambassador for Christ. Her life is a testament that God wastes nothing—not even betrayal—and that He will use the very pain meant to destroy you to build His Kingdom purpose through you.